Original title:
Finding Purpose One Confused Step at a Time

Author: Oliver Bennett
ISBN HARDBACK: 978-1-80566-157-3
ISBN PAPERBACK: 978-1-80566-452-9

Amidst the Chaos

In a world where socks don't pair,
I search for meaning, unaware.
The coffee spills, my shoes untied,
But laughter makes the chaos glide.

Maps are muddled, routes askew,
I chase the wrong bus, what’s my due?
With every stumble, power I gain,
In misadventures, joy I feign.

A Spark Ignites

With every pratfall, wisdom gleams,
Like chasing fireflies in my dreams.
The buttered toast falls to the ground,
But giggles rise, a joyful sound.

A light bulb flickers, ideas bloom,
In tangled thoughts, I find my room.
Through silly slips and goofy spins,
A spark ignites, the laughter wins.

Illuminated by Disarray

The laundry’s mixed, and yet I wear,
A polka-dotted, striped affair.
I dance through life, an awkward grace,
In mayhem’s hug, I find my place.

The path is twisted, full of cheer,
I trip on joy, my vision clear.
In cluttered lanes, I take my flight,
Illuminated by the night.

Tripping Through the Pages of Dreams

I tumble through a book unbound,
With quirky plots and quirks profound.
Each chapter's twist like a misplaced shoe,
In pages turned, I find the clue.

A bookmark's lost, my thoughts adrift,
Each blunder makes my spirits lift.
Through slappy endings, I shall roam,
Tripping on words to call them home.

The Curious Quest of an Aimless Heart

With map in hand and compass broke,
I chase the breeze, I chase the smoke.
A treasure chest of candy bars,
My aimless heart now seeks the stars.

I wander wide with open eyes,
In silly quests, the truth will rise.
Through whimsy's dance and playful part,
I laugh and leap, a happy art.

The Unfolding Map of the Soul's Desire

My map's a scribbled mess of lines,
With arrows pointing everywhere,
I wander on this quest divine,
Where's North? Oh wait, I just don't care!

The coffee shop feels like a shrine,
Offering solace in each sip,
I ponder fate with a dappled vine,
Is curiosity worth the trip?

With every twist, a laugh I chase,
I trip on dreams, I tumble too,
Each tumble leads to a new place,
And sometimes pizza's on the view!

So here I stand, a puzzled chap,
With breadcrumbs leading back to fun,
At least I've mastered the art of nap,
And eating donuts on the run!

Notes from a Wayward Traveler

With suitcase full of lost ideas,
I stroll the streets of ‘I don’t know’,
Each corner hides my hopes and fears,
As I trip on dreams in the flow.

A feather found, a misplaced shoe,
I chart my way on chance and whim,
My playlist's full of songs askew,
But hey, the dance – it’s never grim!

The road sings tales of quirks galore,
With every blunder I embrace,
I juggle life with heaps of lore,
These silly steps, they land with grace.

So here’s to getting lost with glee,
In musty halls of who knows where,
Each laugh a stitch in life's great tapestry,
And joy’s the map I’m proud to bear!

A Compass of Dreams and Doubts

The compass spins like a top so wild,
Its needle winks at fate’s sweet tease,
I’m just a lost and giggling child,
On roads that twist with playful ease.

Each step’s a dance, I trip and jest,
Where logic falters, laughter wins,
I wear my doubts like a party vest,
As tigers dance on paper fins.

The stars are winking from above,
Teasing me with wacky schemes,
While I craft wishes wrapped in love,
Or simply chase inflatable dreams.

So if you see me prance about,
Just know I’m charting paths anew,
With giggles loud, I chase my route,
And in the end, I'll find my crew!

Labyrinthine Paths of the Heart

In corridors of jest and cheer,
I wrangle ghosts of yesteryears,
With each corner, laughter near,
The echoes dance amidst my fears.

I chase my tail like a frisky pup,
With riddles scribbled on a map,
Each twist’s a chance to fill my cup,
And take a little snooze on laps!

The heart's a maze, a playful jest,
Where serendipity takes the lead,
I wear mismatched socks with zest,
And revel in this merry creed.

So come and wander with me a while,
Let’s trip on laughter’s shining art,
Through every twist, we’ll find the style,
And cherish all our goofball hearts!

The Journey Through Winding Labyrinths

In a maze where socks go missing,
I wander through these twists, still hissing.
With each turn, I meet my fate,
And wonder if I am running late.

I tiptoe past a cheese-filled trap,
Then trip over my cat—what a gap!
My compass spins, I can't decide,
If it's lunch or a place to hide.

A sign says ‘this way to the cake’—
I wonder what other paths I make.
With breadcrumbs dropped, I play a game,
My sanity? Well, who's to blame?

The exit’s near, or so they say,
But I'm lost, it’s just another day.
I’ll laugh it off, what can I do?
A life like this is quite the zoo!

Sifting Through Shadows for Clarity

In the dark, where shadows flicker,
I sift through dreams that come much quicker.
With every ghost, I take a leap,
And wonder where my thoughts do creep.

A cat lurks close, with sharpened claws,
As I search for reason, grasping straws.
In corners dark, my doubts take flight,
Like pigeons caught in the dead of night.

I wear a hat that's far too bright,
In hopes it'll guide me home tonight.
But still I twirl, disoriented,
As laughter from ghosts leaves me contented.

At last, I spot a silver beam,
And realize this chaos was just a dream.
With clarity found, I cheer and grin,
In shadows deep, let the fun begin!

The Art of Uncertain Navigation

With a map that looks like ancient art,
I take a deep breath, then start.
The roads twist like a pretzel's twist,
In this adventure, there's much to miss.

Every street sign feels like a joke,
As I stumble upon a goat in smoke.
It bleats directions in riddled rhyme,
Seems my journey will take more time.

A bridge of jelly? I just might cross,
But what if I end up in a frost?
Oh look! A pizza place is near,
Maybe lunch will curb my fear.

The route ahead remains unclear,
But laughter lightens, that's my cheer.
With every wrong turn I take with pride,
In uncertain paths, fun is my guide!

Serendipity Among the Chaos

In a world where plans fall flat,
I trip over cats, what's up with that?
With chaos beckoning at my door,
I step inside, what else is in store?

A blindfold on, I twirl in place,
Is this the new dance or just a chase?
I bump into walls, I hit my head,
Yet here I am, much joy instead.

I find a shoe that’s three sizes wide,
As I stumble out, can't run but glide.
With every slip, I learn to see,
Life’s little surprises dance with glee.

So toss the rules, let’s make a mess,
In serendipity, I'll find success.
With laughter ringing, let chaos bloom,
In my fun-filled life, there’s always room!

The Tapestry of Misguided Adventures

In a land where socks go missing,
A mismatched shoe sparks a dance.
With a hat on my head that's twisted,
I twirl with the hope of a chance.

The map I drew is a riddle,
Leading straight to the café down street.
But I end up lost in a jungle,
Where coffee beans grow on trees to greet.

My compass spins like a record,
As I orbit the same old park.
A squirrel gives me a nod of concern,
While I aim for a home with a spark.

At last, I find my own front door,
With a pizza and lemonade in view.
Misguided? Maybe. But hey,
This adventure is all about you!

A Symphony of Intrigue and Trip-ups

With a kazoo as my conductor,
I march through the arrival surprise.
Each note clashes in joyous chaos,
As folks stop to laugh and to rise.

I search for the golden egg,
But discover an old rubber duck.
It quacks at me in hilarious tones,
Sometimes luck just runs out of luck.

A stumble here, a slide over there,
In a ballet of wobble and spin.
While whispers of wisdom elude me,
I dance with the shadows within.

Yet laughter echoes in the air,
As I trip for what feels like a crime.
Each hiccup transforms my journey,
Into a symphony, uniquely my time!

The Fabric of Curiosity

In a world of mismatched zippers,
Curiosity pulls and tugs.
I chase a peculiar butterfly,
And end up tangled in mugs.

Each bend reveals a new wonder,
Like socks that were deemed long-lost.
With questions that fly like confetti,
I dive in, regardless of cost.

Bumping into a wise old cat,
Who claims to know secrets untold.
Yet when I ask for the meaning,
He trails off, looking so bold.

But laughter blooms like wildflowers,
As I skip along threads of fate.
For sometimes the joy isn't knowing,
But trusting each whim and fate!

Dances with Shadows

In the moonlight's playful embrace,
I twirl with my shadow as friend.
Each misstep a step toward laughter,
Where all awkward trip-ups transcend.

The breeze giggles through the trees,
Whispering secrets of night.
I leap over puddles of doubts,
While my shadow steals the spotlight.

With every stumble, I uncover,
The rhythm of life's wiggly tune.
In foggy lanes where I wander,
Stars join in, a whimsical boon.

So here's to the clumsy, the quirky,
In our dance of unplanned delight.
For every step we keep taking,
Turns the darkness into bright light!

Perception's Path

In shoes too big, I trip and sway,
The signs are blurry, yet I play.
Each zig and zag a chance to laugh,
An awkward dance, my favorite path.

Confused with clues, I grin and roll,
Lost in maps that tease my soul.
A compass set to 'where's the cake?'
I wander on, each step I take.

Puddles splash as I dive right in,
Chasing thoughts that twist and spin.
With every fumble, wisdom grows,
A silly dance, that's how it goes.

So join me on this jumbled way,
Where laughter leads and doubts betray.
With every turn, I'll find my cheer,
A merry journey, my path is clear.

Closer to the Horizon’s Veil

I squint my eyes, the horizon’s near,
But wait… is that a flying deer?
I chase the tales of twilight’s glow,
As shadows whisper secrets low.

With quirky thoughts, I walk my line,
Bumping into clouds of wine.
Each step towards the glow’s delight,
Leads me to giggles in the night.

I juggle dreams and silly schemes,
With every stumble, brightening beams.
Falling stars make wishful lace,
And goofy grins light up my face.

So off I trot, with heart on sleeve,
Toward veils that dance, and then deceive.
In every misstep, joy unfolds,
A journey rich with tales retold.

In the Realm of Fleeting Moments

A twinkling glance, I stop and stare,
Was that a spaceship? No, just air!
Moments flicker like fireflies,
And laughter dangles in the skies.

I trip on thoughts that swirl and spin,
Searching for the entrance within.
With each ‘oops’ comes a radiant grin,
In chaos, that’s where dreams begin.

A butterfly lands upon my nose,
Its tiny wings tell tales of prose.
I dance with time, so fleeting and sweet,
The rhythm of life in my clumsy feet.

So here I stand, in moments brief,
Concocting joy, it’s my chief belief.
With every flicker, I’ll abide,
In this realm where giggles collide.

Treading Water in a Sea of Questions

Floating thoughts like fish in streams,
I paddle forth on silly dreams.
A splash of doubt, a wave of glee,
Caught in questions, can’t you see?

I gulp for air, then sing a tune,
With octopuses under the moon.
Each query bubbles, rises high,
While I splash joy, not asking why.

Fins of fancy, tails that swirl,
In the ocean’s hug, I twirl.
Misunderstood, I ride the tide,
Embracing what the fates decide.

So here I tread, a joyful throng,
In the sea where I belong.
With every ripple, laughter flows,
In waves of questions, who knows?

Moments Bright in the Overcast

I tripped on a banana peel, oh dear,
My shoes still laugh, but I've got cheer.
Clouds above just want to tease,
Yet sunlight dances through the leaves.

A pigeon stole my sandwich today,
I chased it down, but it flew away.
I guess my lunch was just a tease,
But who knew birds would have such ease?

I skipped to avoid a puddle's splash,
Only to land in mud, oh what a crash!
But in the mess, I found a smile,
Laughter echoes down the mile.

With dreams tucked in my socks so snug,
I strut along, a happy bug.
Maybe tripping's part of the game,
In this silly dance, I'll stake my claim.

The Riddle of the Open Road

I took a turn that felt quite bold,
Now I'm lost, or so I'm told.
Maps in hand, I fumble new,
How does one navigate a curlew?

A sign says 'Turn!' but then I blink,
Do I go left, or is that just a wink?
My GPS has lost its mind,
It sends me places I can't find.

Truckers wave as I dance with fate,
They chuckle hard, it's not too late.
Each twist and turn, a comic jest,
Who knew the road could be such a test?

Yet in the chaos, I feel alive,
Weaving tales, my hopes do thrive.
For every misstep on this wide path,
I find my rhythm, and there's my laugh.

In the Wilds of Yearning and Question

In a forest dense with thoughts galore,
I wander aimless to find the core.
Trees whisper secrets, I stop and pause,
What if I'm just a tree in this cause?

Squirrels debate if I'm friend or foe,
Why can't they see I'm here for the show?
With acorns tossed, they spark delight,
While I dance awkwardly, quite a sight!

A rabbit hops, with a knowing nod,
As if to say, 'Don't be so odd!'
But each hop is a lesson learned,
In this funny dance, I've truly yearned.

So I tiptoe on, with laughter and pride,
Among leafy greens, my mayhem's stride.
In the wilds of whims, I'll take my stand,
For in this chaos, I've made my brand.

Where Haze Meets Hope

In the morning mist, I trip and sway,
Coffee in hand, I find my way.
The world spins bright, but here I stay,
Lost in laughter, come what may.

Fog rolled in like a fluffy cloak,
I wave at ghosts and share a joke.
They chuckle back, or so it seems,
In this blurry realm of silly dreams.

A kite goes by, tangled in jests,
It flies past me, on a whim it rests.
'Is that hope?' I shout and cheer,
'Turn it around, and bring it near!'

So I twirl under skies of gray,
With clumsy grace, I'll find my way.
For where the haze meets hopeful hearts,
Life's a canvas, and all are artists.

Chasing Shadows on a Winding Path

I trip on roots and laugh aloud,
My shoe flew off, a dancing crowd.
Around the bend, a squirrel mocks,
As I lose count of all my socks.

The sun is setting, light's a tease,
I'm walking sideways, dodging bees.
Oh look, a sign that points to fun,
But all I see is where I run.

A wild goose chase, or so I thought,
In search of treasure that I sought.
With every twist, I twist my mind,
But in this craziness, joy I find.

So here I roam, a joyful mess,
With silly steps, I do confess.
Each stumble brings a hearty cheer,
As shadows dance, my path is clear.

As the Stars Guide Us Awry

Underneath the twinkling lights,
I question if I'm lost or right.
A map shaped like a pizza slice,
My direction's odd, but oh so nice.

I follow stars that wink and tease,
While tripping over sneaky trees.
A compass spins, it has its whims,
Yet laughter bursts from all my sins.

With every turn, the moon will grin,
A cosmic joke I must begin.
Shall we proceed or risk the night?
With pals like these, it's quite alright.

So here we prance, a cosmic dance,
In confusion, we take a chance.
Each wobbly step is worth the ride,
In newfound joy, we all abide.

Missteps and Mysteries Unfold

With clumsy feet, I stumble through,
Where puzzles lurk, and clues accrue.
A doorbell rings, a cat appears,
I chase it down through fits of cheers.

Beneath the rug, a secret lies,
Perhaps it's just some crumbs, surprise!
Writer's block or jumbled verse,
I chuckle loud, for better or worse.

I chase my thoughts like butterflies,
While tangled thoughts form silly ties.
Each misstep crafts a vibrant tale,
With laughter leading every trail.

So grab your hat, let's skip and hop,
In quirky ways, we'll never stop.
In chaos, find the sweetest thread,
For joy is here, let doubts be shed.

The Heart’s Compass in Turbulent Tides

On wavy shores, my boat's in flux,
Navigating through whale-sized ducks.
The sea is wild, the waves are grand,
Yet laughter sails from my own hand.

While drifting here, I lose my way,
But find a song that wants to play.
With jellyfish that jiggle by,
I raise my cup, and off I fly.

A treasure map with coffee stains,
Where x marks fun, not gold and pains.
Each tide may toss, but spirits soar,
As hearts unlock each open door.

So let the waves take me around,
In playful swells, I’m glory-bound.
In uncertain seas, I find my rhyme,
With every splash, I dance in time.

Notes from a Haphazard Voyage

I set sail on a rubber raft,
With snacks aplenty and dreams unmapped.
The oars are missing, what a laugh,
I'm paddling sideways, call it a craft.

Seagulls mock my flip-flop shoes,
I wave back, spill lemonade, what a muse!
Is this an ocean, or a giant pool?
Diving deep in style, breaking every rule.

Compass spinning like my head,
Is that a mirage, or just my bread?
A map with crayon lines in it, oh dear,
Every turn I take leads to a snack bar near.

So here's to journeys without a plan,
Each misadventure greener than a pan.
Laughing at blunders, I take the plunge,
In the end, is it fun? I solemnly lunge!

Scribbles of a Wayward Dreamer

I dreamed of flying on a pizza slice,
Caught in a tangle of string and ice.
A squirrel gave me directions, all agog,
To find my path through mist and fog.

Bumping into clouds that taste like cheese,
My feet still stuck in last week's sneeze.
Chasing rainbows on roller skates,
What time is it? I've lost all states.

I sketched a treasure map on a napkin,
Every 'X' is a snack I'm stackin'.
With goofy giggles, the sun waves back,
I've misplaced my glasses—wait, they're in my pack!

So here I float, a ship with no sail,
Turning every detour into a tale.
Laughter echoes, and dreams unfold,
With folly in heart, my journey's bold.

Cartography of a Wandering Heart

I’ve got a map drawn by a toddler’s hand,
Each squiggle leads to Cookie Land.
The north is wherever my coffee’s hot,
My instincts say ‘There!’ but get lost a lot.

Every crossroad’s just an ice cream stand,
Heart in a daze, I don’t quite understand.
Then suddenly, a parade of ducks,
Leading me onward, just my luck!

Wanderlust whispers in every crowd,
As I trip over laughter, feeling proud.
With a yellow umbrella spinning in glee,
I’m lost but happy, as happy can be.

Through the mayhem, my spirit roams,
Mapping each giggle, claiming new homes.
In a world of chaos, I make my art,
Each silly moment's a treasure to start.

The Poetry of Missteps

In the dance of life, I’m always off beat,
With two left feet and my lunch as a treat.
Twirl in circles, trip on my dreams,
Yet joy comes quick, bursting at the seams.

A mislaid step, who needs the floor?
I’ll write my own rules, can’t settle for bore.
Salsa with shadows, tango with air,
Every misstep’s a leap, handled with flair.

I fumble with words, a tongue-tied chime,
Yet laughter blossoms, and that's just fine.
As I shuffle in rhythm to my own kind of tune,
Each blunder a blessing, whistling to the moon.

So here’s to the tumble, the fun and the frights,
To the dance of mistakes that spark the delights.
With every trip, I’ll proudly exclaim,
In the poetry of missteps, we all find our fame.

Whispers of Hope in a Foggy Maze

In a maze of socks I wander,
Looking for the matching pair,
I trip on thoughts that slightly ponder,
Is hope hiding underneath a chair?

A fog of dreams, a cloudy mess,
I wave at ghosts of plans gone wrong,
I laugh at fears that cause distress,
In chaos, I still hum my song.

Uncharted Terrain of the Soul

Through jungles thick with self-doubt vines,
I stumble on a hidden stream,
Where every rock is filled with signs,
Directing me to chase a dream.

I map my heart with crayons bright,
In colors that don't always blend,
Each wobbly line's a joyful fight,
A treasure hunt, no start or end.

A Mosaic of Haphazard Steps

With every misstep, I create a scene,
Of chopsticks to eat spaghetti,
Who knew life's dance could be so keen?
I laugh at paths both strange and steady.

Each blunder's just a quirky tile,
In this mosaic of my way,
I'll lean into each silly style,
And find joy in my own ballet.

The Quiet Art of Meandering

I stroll through days like a wayward breeze,
With snacks in hand and silly thoughts,
I stop to pet a friendly tease,
And laugh off what I might have sought.

The winding roads are my delight,
With quirky signs that point to fun,
I twirl beneath the fading light,
And greet the moon, my evening sun.

Beneath the Surface of Misty Wanderings

In the fog, I stumble, trip, and bump,
A chicken dance upon a muddy clump.
I search for signs in clouds that make me grin,
Finding joy in the mess; that's where I'll begin.

Laughter echoes off the trees so wide,
As I chase my shadow, where does it hide?
With pockets full of giggles, I roam,
For every silly step, I feel at home.

Lost my smartphone, but what a view!
The grass tickles my toes as I brew,
A plan to map this wild, wacky spree,
Who needs directions when you have glee?

So here’s to the wanderer with clumsy flair,
Every misstep's a dance, a breath of fresh air.
Underneath it all, fun is my guide,
As I twirl through this life with laughter beside.

Navigating the Unseen Currents

With a compass that spins like a top so wild,
I drift through the woods, somewhat like a child.
Branches grab at my clothes, a slapstick affair,
Yet I giggle aloud without a care!

Direction? Oh, that's just a concept for me,
I follow the ducks, they look so carefree.
If they quack and go left, I'll join in the song,
What's wrong with being lost? It's where I belong!

While everyone else maps out their fate,
I turn every corner, oh isn't it great?
The winds of confusion carry my soul,
In this zany journey, I'm feeling so whole.

So here's to the rivers where no one's in charge,
I'll dance on the banks, living life large.
With each silly step, I just can't deny,
That laughter's my beacon as I fly high!

The Pilgrim's Path of Twists and Turns

Oh, the paths I've trodden are crooked and hilly,
Where each step I take is a somersault silly.
Missed the turn? No matter, I'll wander right here,
Who knew I'd find treasure in moments sincere?

With feet like rubber and a heart made of cheese,
I stumble along while I giggle with ease.
Every twist in the trail is a ticket to play,
And I'm the ringleader in this mad ballet.

My map's upside down, oh what could go wrong?
I'm singing a ditty; the forest sings along.
The squirrels look baffled at my fancy footwork,
While I pirouette past, making them smirk.

So here's to the journey, as offbeat as it seems,
With a dash of absurdity sprinkled in dreams.
For each turn and bend leads to laughter anew,
As I dance on my path, who needs a review?

Footprints on the Edge of Wonder

Each footprint I leave is a giggle, it seems,
Dancing in circles while chasing my dreams.
The ground beneath wobbles like jelly and cream,
With every wrong step, I'm fulfilling a scheme!

I stride on, unkempt with pockets of fun,
While a pair of lost socks gambol under the sun.
The world's my playground, the grass is my stage,
And my wobbly dance moves can't be outdone!

So come take this journey, it's perfectly mad,
There's joy in confusion; you'll never be sad.
With every odd step, a new riddle unfolds,
As I tumble through wonders, both silly and bold.

For when I look back on this whimsical trail,
With laughter and sunshine, I'll never grow pale.
In the end, it's the journey that fills up the heart,
So leap into chaos; it's a marvelous art!

Breadcrumbs of Reflection

With each little crumb that I drop,
I trip over thoughts that just won't stop.
The birds will peck at my trails of doubt,
While I laugh in circles, trying to figure out.

In the forest of chaos, I wander in glee,
Chasing my shadows, but they won't flee.
I dance with the fuzz of uncertainty's breeze,
While squirrels take notes, and I giggle with ease.

Each step feels like running through jelly on toast,
Yet here comes a vision of what I want most.
With rubbery dreams and a squeaky shoe,
I bounce my way back to a world that feels new.

So here's to the crumbs that lead me astray,
They've baked up my journey in a hilarious way.
For in every misstep is laughter to find,
A treasure of silliness, whiskey in mind.

The Alchemy of Mist and Intention

In a foggy lab of muddled ideas,
I mix up ambitions with unnecessary fears.
With a wink and a nod, I'll stir up a brew,
Of coffee and chaos, and hope it's not stew.

I sprinkle some giggles, add a dash of grace,
And watch as the potion makes a silly face.
The beakers are bubbling with laughter and light,
While I navigate this hilarious plight.

With diluted desires evaporating fast,
I cotton-candy hop over a question-mark cast.
"Why am I here?" in a lab coat of dreams,
I giggle aloud as the universe beams.

So here in this chaos, I mix up my fate,
With a pinch of absurdity, it's never too late.
For the secret to life hides in laughter so free,
In the alchemy of nonsense, I dance with great glee.

Mirage of a Steady Horizon

I chase after sunsets that slip right away,
They shimmer and wiggle, all dressed in decay.
"Steady," I mumble, while tripping on fluff,
The horizon laughs back, "You're never enough!"

Each step on this journey feels slightly off-kilter,
Like wearing a hat made of scrambled eggs, glitter.
The mirage winks slyly as I start to jiggle,
I'm lost in the fog, but still start to wiggle.

With every new path that appears in the mist,
I ponder the purpose of dreams I've dismissed.
But the laughter that follows keeps calling me home,
And I dance to the echo of a whimsical foam.

So here's to the vistas that tease and confuse,
I'll skip down this trail in my mismatched shoes.
For the horizon may bend, but my heart expands wide,
In the mirage of laughter, I'll always abide.

The Gift of Detours

On a winding road where the signs are a joke,
I keep bumping into my whims and a poke.
With each silly turn and a left when I'd right,
Life gifts me detours wrapped up in pure light.

The GPS gives up, and so do I,
As I follow the birds that are all flying high.
With a giggle I dart from the path I once knew,
Becoming a tourist in a world that feels new.

I stumble on treasures where I never would look,
A rainbow, a unicorn, and an old history book.
Wandering further, I marvel and muse,
Each twist in the trail is the best kind of fuse.

So bring on the detours, the laughter they bring,
Unraveled confusions, like a broken string.
For life's greatest gifts are the ones you don't plan,
In the joy of the journey, I'm the happiest fan.

Uncharted Steps Beneath a Starless Sky

With socks that clash and shoes untied,
I stumble forth, a dorky guide.
The moon's on strike, the stars forgot,
But hey, at least, I found a lot!

I trip on thoughts that twist and flop,
The path I choose? A total bop!
Each step I take, I trip and cheer,
My inner compass disappears!

I juggle dreams like balls in air,
They fly around without a care.
If success is close, why can't I feel?
That silly feeling of surreal!

But in the chaos, giggles bloom,
A dance with fate in this vast room.
Each tumble and twist, a tale to tell,
Of starless nights that go so well!

The Puzzle of a Roaming Spirit

In a maze of thoughts that twist and twine,
I chase my mind like it's a feline.
Each corner turned, I lose my way,
But hey! It's just another day.

A jigsaw piece my coffee spilled,
A laugh erupts, enthusiasm filled.
With every sip a puzzle made,
I'm best with chaos on parade!

A cat that purrs, my trusted muse,
In whimsy's grasp, I just can't lose.
Each misfit moment, a mystery bright,
Who knew confusion could feel so light?

So here's to wandering spirits free,
Let's dance to tunes of hilarious glee.
In this puzzled scheme, we roam and play,
Where nothing's clear, but that's okay!

Lost and Found in the Chronicles of Self

In the library of my own mind's play,
I search for wisdom in yesterday.
With dusty books and covers torn,
A rebel bard has been reborn!

I wear mismatched shoes, it’s my grand style,
As I wander through this info aisle.
If life's a quest, I'm on chapter ten,
Lost and found, again and again.

Each page I turn, it flutters wide,
Filled with typos in every stride.
But here’s the twist—who really cares?
They are my footprints, my own pair!

So let's read on with gleeful sighs,
In jumbled tales, the laughter lies.
For as I fumble, I start to see,
The greatest story is just me!

Intersections of the Untamed Mind

At the crossroads where thoughts collide,
A squirrel dances, it's my guide.
Should I go left or take a right?
I'll toss a coin; it feels just right!

With thoughts like confetti, they swirl around,
I trip on ideas scattered on the ground.
But oh! The joy in every fall,
My brain's a party, come one, come all!

Maps are for folks who know their way,
I scribble routes on a cocktail tray.
With mixed-up plans, I'm sure to collide,
But what's adventure without a wild ride?

So here I stand, a jester and king,
With my thoughts as my crown, I laugh and sing.
In the untamed wild of my mind's expanse,
I blooper my way through life's silly dance!

The Compass of Uncertainty

My compass spins like a disco ball,
Pointing wherever it may call.
I chase the North, but face the West,
In this dizzy dance, I do my best.

With each wrong turn, I simply laugh,
Who needs a map? I'll draw a giraffe.
I'll waltz on paths that twist and bend,
Embrace the chaos; it's my new friend.

A treasure hunt for socks and dreams,
Or maybe just lost ice cream themes.
I stumble on rocks, roll like a ball,
At least I'm moving, or so I call.

So here I am, in this wacky quest,
With a compass that suggests I rest.
I'll follow the giggles, the snorts, and the cries,
And who knows? I might just reach the skies.

In Search of Tomorrow's Echo

I asked the dawn for a little hint,
But it just chuckled, 'Go take a sprint!'
With sunshine on my mismatched shoes,
I’ll race the squirrels; they can’t refuse.

The future’s dressed like a clown today,
With polka dots and a bright array.
I trip and tumble, but always grin,
For the echoes of laughter drown the din.

A map of clouds leads the way to fun,
Or was it spaghetti? Either will run!
I’ll chase the echoes with a silly cheer,
While the echoes giggle, “We’re already here!”

So here’s my dance in the morning light,
In search of tomorrows that feel so right.
With each footstep, I’ll sing and sway,
Tomorrow, come out; I’m on my way!

Wandering in the Mist

In morning mist, I lose my sight,
But I'm still here, and that feels right.
I bump into trees, and they don't mind,
As they whisper secrets that I won't find.

With foggy logic, I skip and hop,
Every cloud a bus stop, a lemonade shop.
I ask the wind for directions true,
It just giggles and says, "What's new?"

I search for signs like a blindfolded cat,
Only to find a misplaced hat.
But who needs clarity when jesters play?
I'll waddle through life; it's a fun ballet.

So I dance in the mist with glee untold,
Collecting memories, both faint and bold.
In wanderings lost, I've found a clue,
That laughter is the map; it leads me through.

Footprints on the Pathless Trail

Each step I take, a giggle burst,
On a winding road that's quite a first.
With footprints left in jelly and cream,
I'm crafting my path from a silly dream.

The trail is wild, a picnic spread,
With peanut butter and dreams misled.
I follow ants with tiny caps,
Through zigzag rights and backward laps.

No signposts here, just clouds afloat,
Each nook a talking, singing goat.
With every stomp, the world feels grand,
As I twirl and float on this whimsy land.

So onward I wander, with giggles in tow,
On this pathless trail where few dare go.
With jelly footprints, I'll dance with glee,
For the journey's the treasure where I'll be free.

Chasing Dreams in Circles

I chased a dream while tripping on my shoelace,
A goal so bright, yet I lost my own pace.
I ran around in arcs, just like a hound,
Barking at the moon, still nowhere to be found.

Each step I took felt like a silly dance,
With every stutter, I'd give fate a glance.
Juggling thoughts like eggs upon a spoon,
Wondering if I'd find it all by noon.

The world spins fast, while I walk in place,
A merry-go-round, a comical race.
I spun and grinned, just enjoying the ride,
Who needs a map when you've got this side?

So here I stand, a circus act of fate,
Wobbling on the line, it's never too late.
With laughter loud, and a heavy stance,
I'll turn this chaos into a chance to dance.

Unraveled Threads of Destiny

I knitted dreams with yarn made of fluff,
But tangled up my thoughts—oh, that was tough.
With needles in hand, I pricked at my heart,
Wondering when this chaos would start.

A tapestry of wishes, all knotted and spliced,
Every stitch a moment, not all were precise.
I yanked on a thread and the whole thing fell,
Did I create art, or just make a spell?

With every loop, I'd laugh at the mess,
The fabric of life, it's anyone's guess.
A patchwork of choices, both grand and absurd,
Stitched together by actions, each sloppily blurred.

So let's unravel this colorful plight,
I'll wear my confusion like a favorite fright.
In patterns of laughter, I'll wade through the fray,
Hand-stitched adventures will brighten the day.

The Dance of Hesitant Hopes

I took a step, then shuffled right back,
My feet had a mind of their own, quite the knack.
In a jitterbug jig, I spun through the air,
With every uncertain twirl, I shed my despair.

A cha-cha of choices, a waltz of the weird,
Each misstep I took was somehow revered.
I bailed on the beat, but found my own tune,
As laughter echoed, I danced with the moon.

The rhythm of life is a tricky charade,
With flailing limbs in an awkward parade.
But who needs perfection when laughter ignites?
Every blunder is precious, in colorful lights.

So here's my refrain, a toe-tapping cheer,
In the dance of my doubts, I'll persevere.
For every misstep is a part of the song,
In this funny ballet, we all can belong.

Whispers from the Kaleidoscope

I peered through the lens of a glassy delight,
Captured visions of nonsense, in colors so bright.
Twists of reality twinkled with flair,
Each twist and each turn was beyond compare.

Glimpses of life spun in riotous hues,
Confusion wrapped lightly, like sparkly shoes.
I giggled at thoughts, all jumbled like cheese,
A feast for the brain that was sure to please.

In this whirl of laughter, meaning would creep,
Dancing with dreams that tumble and leap.
The chaotic patterns we weave in our mind,
Bring joy in the journey, so beautifully blind.

So come take a peek, let's whirl through the fun,
In a kaleidoscope world, we're never quite done.
With whispers of whimsy and stories untold,
Let's cherish the laughter, let the colors unfold.

In Search of Echoes

In the forest of my mind, I roam,
Chasing shadows, lost with a gnome.
He claims he knows the way to go,
But every path smells like old toe.

I asked the moon for a little light,
But she just giggled and took to flight.
With whispers of wisdom, I sought the wise,
Turns out, they're just great at telling lies.

Chickens cross roads, I cross my heart,
Each step feels like a work of art.
Why can't I find a GPS for laughs?
Every wrong turn, just adds to my gaffs.

So here I stand with my rubber feet,
Lost in a world that smells like feet.
Echoes of laughter, the best kind of sound,
In confusion, I dance round and round.

Poised on the Brink of the Unforeseen

I’m dangling on a tightrope of fate,
With one shoe on, feeling first-rate.
The crowd below, they munch on popcorn,
I scream, 'Is this what I was born?'

Balancing thoughts like a wobbly cake,
The fork in my path is a serious mistake.
Should I jump left or do a little spin?
You'd think with all this, I’d surely win.

Every option’s a jigsaw, missing some parts,
Yet I’m piecing together all of my arts.
I met a cat, it gave me a wink,
Said, 'Life’s like a fish that just can’t think.'

But here I am, still chasing the breeze,
With mismatched socks, and knees like cheese.
Who knew the brink could feel so absurd?
I take a leap and let dreams be stirred.

The Canvas of Choices Under Starlit Skies

With paintbrush in hand, I start to sway,
Mixing my choices in a colorful way.
Stars up above, they wink and joke,
As I create from dreams and smoke.

The colors swirl, yellow and blue,
Each stroke a mishap, but who knew?
A giraffe on a bicycle rides by,
Whispering, 'Darling, give it a try!'

Confetti the size of my wildest dreams,
Sprinkles of life in magical themes.
But who needs a plot? It's chaos, hooray!
I'll paint my own path in my quirky way.

The canvas may splatter, but that's just fine,
Each smudge reveals the joy that's mine.
Under the stars, I'll scribble some more,
For each quirky choice, opens a door.

Each Step, A Painting of Possibility

With each tiny step, I trip and twirl,
Like a clumsy dancer in a crazy whirl.
My feet are paintbrushes, the ground is a stage,
I toss my worries, unleash my rage.

Sketching my path in silly delight,
Each foot falls boldly, fighting the fright.
A banana peel here, a giggle from there,
Life's just a circus, without a care!

A dance with the wind, a hop with a cheer,
As I spill my thoughts, simple and clear.
Who needs a map? Just follow the fun,
Lost is the new found, and we've just begun.

So let's laugh and wobble, embrace the bizarre,
Every step we take feels like a shooting star.
In this crazy art show, where blunders abound,
Each painted step spills magic on the ground.

The Mutable Path of Self-Discovery

In search of shoes that fit just right,
I tripped on wisdom, not quite bright.
Each misstep danced like it's a dream,
As I navigated life's wobbly beam.

A compass pointing every which way,
It laughed out loud, like it's on display.
With map in hand, I crossed some streams,
In puddles of purpose, I lost my dreams.

Yet laughter echoed through the air,
As I sculpted moments without a care.
Each tumble led to newfound cheer,
Confusion, it seems, was a friend quite dear.

So twirl and swirl on this path of fun,
As I fumble toward the rising sun.
With every giggle, I take a chance,
The dance of life is a clumsy prance.

Afterglow of Confusion's Embrace

With eyes wide shut, I took a leap,
Into the realms of dreams so deep.
Confusing colors, shapes that flow,
Yet somewhere in here, I'd find my glow.

A pizza slice shaped like a cat,
Why not, I thought, I'll wear that hat!
In whirlwinds of laughter, I spun around,
Each silly mishap in joy was found.

The aftershocks of a puzzling race,
Left me grinning, embracing the space.
For every wrong turn, the right made sense,
My mixed-up path, a cute recompense.

Embracing chaos, I will shout,
For joy lurks here, without a doubt.
With giggles echoing through my mind,
In the clouds of confusion, purpose I'll find.

Kaleidoscope of Wandering Thoughts

A whirl like a kaleidoscope spins,
An odd mix of loss and silly wins.
Each thought a color, swirling bright,
In this merry maze, I search for light.

With every twist, the scene would change,
Like socks that dance, how they arrange!
In patterns skewed yet oh so fun,
Serendipity sings as I start to run.

I wrote a plan, then tossed it away,
For laughter leads me astray and play.
Each slippery slope a footloose song,
In this playful state, I truly belong.

So gather up all these thoughts that bounce,
They jiggle and wriggle, they laugh and pounce.
In this whirlwind
of delightful surprise,
I'll find my way through comedic skies.

The Speech of Silent Journeys

Amidst the whispers of secret quests,
I strolled where silence wore funny vests.
Each step a chuckle, a bemused sigh,
In this wordless talk, how time does fly!

With shoes untied, my feet set free,
I meandered forth, planning to be.
Yet on the trail, my thoughts would slip,
Like yogurt on toast, soft and flip.

A stray dog giggled, chuffed with glee,
"I've no directions, come follow me!"
Through meadows of mischief and fields of jest,
In this quiet stroll, I felt so blessed.

And in the end, it's not the speech,
But how to dance when life's out of reach.
With laughter ringing in the morning's dew,
I chuckle at all the wrongs that felt true.

A Spiral of Steps toward Tomorrow

In flip-flops I wander, so lost in my mind,
With each wobbly step, my true path I'll find.
The grass tickles toes, as I teeter and sway,
But laugh at the journey, come what may!

A squirrel shimmies past, with a nut in its mouth,
I pause for a moment, then head further south.
Oh look, there's a fountain! I think it's divine,
But all I can think is, where'd I put my line?

Around every corner, a puzzling new sight,
Like juggling spaghetti in the broad daylight.
I slip on a banana, it’s comedy gold,
Life hands me lemons, but hey, I’m still bold!

So onward I trot, with a smile on my face,
Stumbling in style, it’s a curious race.
Each misstep a story, in this grand little show,
I’ll twirl and I’ll twist, like a sunflower's glow!

Dissonance and Harmony Like Puzzles

A puzzle of socks sprawls across the floor,
One's blue, one’s green, and I’m still wanting more.
I scratch my head hard, none match in a row,
Will I ever find joy in this sock overload?

A cat leaps in, and the chaos ignites,
Chasing those mismatched delights in mid-flight.
I laugh as it tumbles, my feline expert,
In this puzzling mess, I’m the real concert!

Jigsaw of mornings, can’t find a clear plan,
But let’s flip the pieces, a whimsical fan.
With each jumbled thought, a chuckle to share,
I play with the dissonance, without a care!

So here’s to the mix-ups, the ups and the downs,
In this slapstick ballet, where everyone frowns.
We dance in confusion, find rhythm in strife,
And turn mismatched socks into a colorful life!

The Clay of Uncertainties Crafted

With hands full of clay, I mold out a dream,
But it falls every time—it's not as it seems.
A squishy distraction, it shapes on its own,
I guess it has thoughts, my mind has outgrown!

A wobbly figure, am I sculpting a duck?
Or maybe a masterpiece—hmmm, who gives a pluck?
I laugh at the chaos, my heart starts to race,
As my pot becomes more of a comical face.

Each twist is a giggle, a slip and a slide,
I'm just here to play, not win at the ride.
Let the clay do the talking, it's not just in hands,
The joy of the journey's where true magic stands!

So bring on the ooze and the messy delight,
With each groan and chuckle, my spirit takes flight.
In this clay of confusion, my colors entwine,
Crafting silly wonders, out of a crooked line!

A Symphony of Compass Roses

My compass spins wildly, it refuses to rest,
Pointing to donuts, oh what a jest!
In search of direction, I follow my nose,
But wind up at a circus, where a clown overthrows!

A dance in the chaos, I juggle my fate,
This prized compass guide said, 'Don’t hesitate!'
I stumble through laughter, my plans go awry,
With a pie in my face, I can only comply.

The roses all spin, in a whimsical turn,
As I follow my gut, and my tummy does yearn.
A game of confusion, but who really knows,
If the magic is there, in the path that I chose?

So tune into the nonsense, the merry and wild,
For joy is the answer, the spirit of a child.
In this quirky symphony, I dance through the mess,
And here’s to the journey—I’ll always confess!

A Tale of Tangents and Turns

Once I took a left, then a right,
Did a jig on the street, what a sight!
A parade of pigeons joined my dance,
With my sense of direction, I stood no chance.

I asked a cat for directions, quite absurd,
It just meowed back, wouldn't say a word.
Chasing my tail, like a dizzy old fool,
Turns out GPS can be a one-way tool.

Each corner I turned held a new surprise,
Found a donut shop—oh, the sugary pies!
Got lost in the laughter, the joy of the chase,
In the maze of confusion, I found my place.

So here I am, with a smile so wide,
Lost but delighted on this bumpy ride.
Every twist that I take leads to more fun,
In the tale of my life, I'm the star of the run.

Through the Mist of Unfamiliar Streets

Fog rolling in like a thick woolly spree,
I stumbled upon a dog—had a global degree!
He wagged his little tail, offered me a grin,
I followed him closely, where do I fit in?

Map upside down, I twist and I twirl,
Is that a bakery, or just a squirrel?
Every step a gamble, a bet gone awry,
Hoping the next corner won’t make me cry.

Passing through flavors, sweet, spicy, and bold,
Each alley a whisper, a tale to be told.
Lost in the laughter of wandering folks,
I trip over moments, they’re my funny jokes.

With every misstep, I dance and I sway,
Through unfamiliar streets, I’m here to play.
The fog lifts gently, revealing the sun,
And in this great maze, I'm the jester who won.

The Soliloquy of a Lost Traveler

Oh, where am I going? My map's out of whack,
Walked into a bakery, now I'm covered in snacks.
I'll chart my own course through pancakes and pies,
With syrupy smiles and a side of surprise.

A compass is nice, but I've lost its charm,
My feet have their own plans, they're filled with alarm.
Do I turn left or just keep going straight?
Decisions are hard when you're juggling your fate.

A squirrel tries to help, but he's chasing a nut,
I laugh at the chaos, life's one big glut.
Trying to find logic in my haphazard dance,
In the voiceless adventures, I take my chance.

So here's to the wanderers, the wayward souls,
Who trip on their laces and stumble on goals.
With laughter as my guide, I'm taking the lead,
In the soliloquy of life, confusion's my creed.

The Heart’s Song in the Midst of Confusion

In a world of directions, I’m dancing offbeat,
Lost in a melody of mismatched feet.
My heart sings a chorus of giggles and quirks,
As I whirl like a leaf in the park while it works.

Each turn is a stanza, each wrong way a rhyme,
I’ll disco through life—what a wonderful time!
The streetlights are singing, the shadows they sway,
In the heart’s dance of chaos, I’ll twirl and play.

A symphony of mischief, I embrace the weird,
In paths uncharted, my spirit has cheered.
Every wrong turn leads to laughter anew,
In this whimsical journey, I’ve found my true view.

So let the roads twist like pretzels today,
With a heart full of rhythm, I’m finding my way.
In the midst of confusion, I’m singing out loud,
For every lost traveler, let’s celebrate proud.

The Threads We Weave along the Way

In a world of tangled strings,
I trip on my shoelace while the cat sings.
Every loop I tie propels me forth,
Yet my coffee spills, it's the world's worth.

A compass spins wild, there's no clear north,
The GPS says 'Turn left!' but I veer forth.
With every step, I dance like a clown,
An acorn falls, and I tumble down.

Friends join in with a waltz on the grass,
Each misstep leads to a giggle, alas!
We draw new paths with chalk on the street,
While mapping out dreams beneath our feet.

So here's to the joy of getting lost,
In puddles of laughter, no matter the cost.
Through misadventures, we weave our way,
With threads of love that will never fray.

Muddled Maps and Heartfelt Yearnings

I consult my map, but it’s upside down,
The X I seek just points to a frown.
A hot dog stand? Well, that’s a delight,
I’ll find my way home with mustard tonight.

Balloons in the air, trying to fly,
My shoes squeak loudly as birds pass by.
Each step is a dance, awkward and free,
As I do the cha-cha with a neighbor's bee.

Guide me, oh stars, with your glittery flaws,
While I chase my dreams on all fours and paws.
I stumble and tumble, but giggles remain,
In this game of life where I entertain.

So let’s raise a toast to the silly and strange,
To the muddled paths that cause a change.
In laughter, I find where my bliss is tossed,
Turns out the journey is worth every loss.

Footfalls on the Fringe of Clarity

In shoes too big, I clomp and sway,
Each step I take leads me astray.
I trip on thoughts, they tumble out,
While pigeons laugh, they strut about.

My map's a doodle, directions wrong,
A route that's more like a silly song.
I wander forth, like a lost balloon,
With every misstep, I hum a tune.

The pavement whispers, "Just go and play,"
So onward I charge, come what may.
The fringe of sense, a wobbly line,
Where clarity hides, all drunk on wine.

Yet every stumble brings me cheer,
A dance of chaos—joy draws near.
With each footfall, I laugh, I grin,
Confusion's my friend; let the fun begin!

The Puzzle of My Disordered Steps

With pieces missing, the jigsaw's bare,
I skip and hop without a care.
My toes are cold, my socks mismatched,
A quirky dance that feels detached.

I juggle thoughts like circus clowns,
One falls away, another drowns.
I'm piecing dreams, all upside down,
With silly faces, I wear a frown.

A step to the left, now to the right,
It seems my compass lost its sight.
But giggles bubble within the fuss,
As laughter rings like a circus bus.

So bring on chaos, I say with glee,
For life's a puzzle, just let it be.
My disordered steps create a dance,
In a world that spins, I'll take my chance!

Caresses of the Uncertain Breeze

The wind has jokes it likes to share,
Whispering secrets and tossing my hair.
I drift like a leaf, twirling up high,
With every gust, I bump a passerby.

Like a kite on a string, I float confound,
With no clear path, I'm blissfully found.
The breeze pulls me left, then spins me right,
Oh, what a whirl! What a silly flight!

I chase after clouds, but they tease and flee,
While I chase my thoughts like they're fish in the sea.
Uncertain and wobbly, I frolic with ease,
In the warm embrace of the playful breeze.

Each gust a giggle, each swirl a grin,
In this topsy-turvy world, let the fun begin.
For as long as I sway with laughter in tow,
The caresses of wind just help me grow!

How the Heart Knows the Way

My heart runs wild like a puppy untrained,
It jumps, it barks, in joy it’s unchained.
While my brain flips through the busy brochure,
My heart says, "Go!"—and what's there to ignore?

With fuzzy maps and a compass of dreams,
It leads me through life’s bizarre schemes.
I dance in the chaos, so light on my toes,
Hurdling through life as it whimsically flows.

With every detour and twist in the lane,
I giggle at mishaps—no room for disdain.
For every wrong turn is a tale to regale,
In laughter, I find my very own trail.

So here’s to my heart and its curious sway,
It knows where to go, come whatever may.
In this humorous journey, like cats on parade,
I’ll skip with a chuckle, unafraid, unafraid!

The Threads of Errant Dreams

I tripped over my sleepy thoughts,
Fell into a pile of socks,
Chasing fluff, dreams wait in knots,
Laughter echoes from old blocks.

Lost my way in a cereal bowl,
Counted spoons instead of stars,
Navigating with a brimming soul,
Yet I'm stuck in my pajamas.

A rubber duck leads my parade,
Waddling through life's curvy maze,
Each quack a cheer, a sweet charade,
As I dance in a dizzy haze.

So I'll stitch these moments tight,
With mismatched threads, bold and bright,
Turning chaos into delight,
Finding sparkles in my flight.

Explorations in the In-Between

In between the sips of tea,
Lies a world of laughter's trace,
I doodle plans to be quite free,
But end up in a shoe's embrace.

Maps designed by a toddler's hand,
With arrows pointing at the fridge,
Wonders wait at snack time’s stand,
While I consider jumping a bridge.

A sandwich speaks of journeys grand,
With mustard maps and pickle dreams,
Every bite an unplanned strand,
Unraveling in crumbly schemes.

So here I float, a silly kite,
In windy whims, I take to flight,
Exploring edges, feeling right,
In this dance of laugh and light.

Shifts of Direction in a Sea of Questions

Oh, which way do I even go?
Directions swirl like cheese fondue,
As thoughts play hide and seek below,
I follow crumbs left by a shoe.

The compass spins, makes me dizzy,
Should I chase that barking cat?
As I ponder if this is easy,
I trip on dreams, and down I splat!

My GPS lost in culinary realms,
Pizza leads me off the path,
While spaghetti sways like phantom helms,
I'm caught in a noodle's wrath.

Yet laughter bubbles from my heart,
As I navigate this playful art,
Each question's just a funky start,
In a dance where joy takes part.

Edges Softened by Unanswered Whispers

A whisper floats on avocado toast,
It beckons me to take a bite,
How can I even hear it boast,
While debating if I’m quite right?

The shadows shift, a game of peek,
Answers hide behind the cracks,
My mind’s a circus, or a freak,
As I wrestle with my little snacks.

The silence sings a playful tune,
As I juggle thoughts of lost cues,
Guess I’ll just dance beneath the moon,
With a hat that's made of pinked blues.

So here I twirl, with giggles gleamed,
In the edges where questions shy,
Softened by the dreams I've dreamed,
With a belly laugh and a winked eye.

Embracing the Riddle of Now

I woke up today, my socks don't match,
Chasing dreams that seem to scratch.
Lost in the maze of my own design,
Is that a snack, or is it just a sign?

I dance with doubt, my steps askew,
A caterpillar in a tutu.
With every stumble, I laugh and fall,
Maybe there's sense wrapped in it all.

So I twirl like a top, dizzy with fun,
Wearing mismatched socks under the sun.
Embracing the riddle, I take a bow,
Who really knows what's in store for me now?

Through fun and confusion, I find my way,
Maybe it's chicken or maybe it's clay.
Life's only a puzzle wrapped in a jest,
And I'm giggling my way to the next quirky quest.

Echoes of a Stumbling Heart

I walked outside, tripped on a dream,
In a world that sparkles and sometimes screams.
Duck or turkey, I can't decide,
As I tumble through life on this wild, crazy ride.

My heart's a drummer, missing the beat,
Yet I shuffle along with two left feet.
Each step a giggle, each fall a song,
Who knew confusion could feel so strong?

Picking up treasures from the floor,
Is that my lunch? Oh, what’s the score?
Echoes of laughter as I trip and glide,
Every misstep a reason to stride.

In this dance of chaos, I find my tune,
A wobbly waltz beneath the moon.
Stumbling through life with silly delight,
Why not be lost on this merry night?

Mosaic of a Meandering Soul

In the yard, I spotted a bright red shoe,
Wondering if it once belonged to you.
A garden gnome waves, or is it a wink?
What do I wear? Oh, what do you think?

My thoughts like marbles, rolling around,
A treasure hunt just waiting to be found.
Each scatter and shuffle reveals a part,
A mosaic unfolding from my clumsy heart.

Seeking the sparkle in every mishap,
I giggle and tumble, wear my own map.
What seems a blunder turns gold in the light,
My meandering soul is a curious sprite.

So here's to the quirks and the laughter they bring,
Life spins like a record, always on bling.
In this wild serenade, I dance all around,
A jigsaw of joy, where confusion is found.

The Light Amidst the Fog

I wandered into the woods filled with haze,
Lost in my thoughts, caught in a daze.
A bear in pajamas passed right on by,
Is it a sighting? Should I wave or cry?

The trees sigh softly, sharing their views,
As I trip on twigs and revel in blues.
With each foggy step, a chuckle or two,
The light beckons softly, but oh, where are you?

Sometimes I fumble, but laughter breaks through,
The trees have their stories, and I have a few.
Waving at shadows, I trip, yet I grin,
The bright light ahead is where I begin.

So I dance in the mist, a shimmering sprite,
Hoping to stumble upon something bright.
With joy as my compass, I stride through the grey,
In this foggy adventure, I'm finding my way.

Discoveries in the Half-Light

In shadows where the lost socks roam,
I tripped on dreams I thought were gone.
A dance of dust, a tumble and twirl,
Just me and my shoes in a quirky swirl.

With a map made of napkins, I stride so bold,
Chasing my thoughts like a game of chess.
Left foot, then right, oh what a joy!
Mind's playground, it's all just a mess.

A cat on the prowl gives me a wink,
As I step on a puddle, what do you know?
The universe laughs, drinks tea with a clink,
In this whimsical world, I'm the star of the show.

With giggles and guffaws, away I go,
In this half-light, where the sillies abound.
Every misstep a miracle, you know!
In each little hiccup, pure gold can be found.

The Map of an Unmapped Journey

With arrows that point where I have not been,
I wander through forests of socks and old jeans.
Maps lead me nowhere, yet here I remain,
Sketching my dreams with a splash of disdain.

This pathless path has me singing loud,
Reciting my woes to a passing cloud.
Every rustle of leaves, a venture unwound,
In a world upside down, where clowns are profound.

With each quirky turn, I often collide,
Bumping the hedges while trying to hide.
The thorns sing my praises, the weeds roll their eyes,
In this topsy-turvy, hilarious guise.

I'm lost, but I'm laughing, what more could I need?
With pinches of joy, all I do is succeed.
This map made of giggles guides my merry way,
In the chaos of laughter, I dance and I sway.

Scribbles of the Wandering Heart

My heart writes in scribbles, all jumbled and wild,
Like a toddler who drives with a grin and a smile.
Each line a mistake, yet still I embrace,
The doodles of life, my favorite place.

Every pothole I hit is a story to tell,
Turned upside down, and I still feel swell.
In shambles I gather my scattered confetti,
As the stars in my eyes shine bright and unsteady.

A funny old bird cackles from a tree,
Joining my journey with laughter and glee.
With each goofy step, I twirl in delight,
In this wobbly waltz, I take flight in the night.

With crayon-thoughts on a canvas so grand,
I paint with my heart, no borders, no plan.
In doodles and humor, I make my own art,
Joyously scribbling the path of my heart.

Writing New Chapters in the Unknown

With a quill made of spaghetti, I scribble the tale,
Of a journey untraveled, where giggles prevail.
Each line is a noodle, twirled up in delight,
Crafting chapters of chaos, oh what a sight!

I'm penning my story on fortune's whim,
In pages of mush, let the laughter begin.
Every misadventure a chapter unfolds,
With toppings of whimsy in great heaps and folds.

Through coffee spills and late-night ice cream,
I'm scripting my life like a wild, wacky dream.
A rubber duck narrator quacks out the plot,
As I dance through the unknown, tangled but hot!

Each footstep a plot twist, a wrinkle in time,
I’m turning the pages with rhythm and rhyme.
With a grin on my face, I'll embrace every flaw,
In this book of the baffled, I’m laughing in awe.

www.ingramcontent.com/pod-product-compliance
Lightning Source LLC
Chambersburg PA
CBHW051629160426
43209CB00004B/571
* 9 7 8 1 8 0 5 6 6 1 5 7 3 *